"But he answered and said, It is written, Man shall not live by bread alone, but by every word that proceedeth out of the mouth of God."
Matthew 4:4

International COOKBOOK RECIPES

Authentic Home Recipes From Around The World And Testimonies From Radio Listeners And Students From Many Foreign Countries.

Dr. Johnny Woodard~DD

For more information about the Bread Of Life International Bible Correspondence Institute, we can be contacted at the information given below.

The Bread Of Life International
Bible Correspondence Institute
P.O. Box 334
Kirbyville, Texas
75956

bolbcs@gmail.com

http://www.simplesite.com/

Foreword

On that beautiful August night in Jerusalem while looking down on the Old City Of Jerusalem from the Mount Of Olives with Dr. Jack Meeks, I had no idea of the tremendous opportunity to reach multitudes with God's Word that was about to be given to me. It was on that last night of the Israel mission trip that Dr. Jack Meeks asked me if I would be interested in teaching Bible prophecy on his Bread Of Life Victory Hour radio broadcast. I told him I would pray about it and get back with him. After returning home, my wife Jewel and I, after much prayer told Dr. Meeks we felt sure that God was leading us to work with him and The Bread Of Life Baptist Fellowship and I began speaking on his worldwide radio broadcast.

Not long after that Dr. Meeks asked me if I would take over The Bread Of Life International Bible Correspondence Institute. We agreed and started doing some deputation to help raise funds needed to mail out the Bible lessons around the world. To make a long story short, I later on designed all the Bible Study lessons for our school and we have seen it grow tremendously since that time in 1996.

Through the years some of our radio listeners would send in home recipes and I would save them. Much later on I decided to put together a cookbook with these home recipes, which are in this book. They are exactly as they were sent to us. We have only used one of the recipes in the book, that being the Mexican Chili and it was the best we ever tasted. All the texts are in English, but some of the measurements are not what we commonly use.

I have also included some of the hundreds and hundreds of testimonies I have received through the years in this book. When I first began working with Dr. Meeks and started getting letters from foreign lands, I was shocked at what was taking place around the world. I was contacted with a tremendous amount of requests for Bibles and other Gospel materials. I also was moved by the personal stories of persecution many of our fellow believers were facing. This book contains only a few of the thousands of testimonies I have received through the years. I pray everything in this book will be a blessing and an inspiration to you. No part of this book can be used for personal gain or commercial purposes but can be used freely as the Lord leads.

Dr. Johnny Woodard
President

Index

Algeria	1
Argentina	2
Azerbaijan	5
Brazil	6
Cambodia	11
Canary Islands	12
China	13
Columbia	14
Congo	15
Croatia	18
El Salvador	20
Greenland	21
Honduras	22
Indonesia	23
Mexico	27
Nigeria	28
Pakistan	29
Peru	30
Russia	31
Serbia	32
Slovenia	33
Ukraine	34
Testimonies	35
CD Ministry	56

Algeria Onion Bread

Ingredients

2 Tablespoons active dry yeast
3/4/cup warm water
3 tablespoons sugar (divided)
2 cups water
2 teaspoons of salt
3 tablespoons softened margarine
6 ¼ to 6 ¾ cups of sifted flour1
1- 1 ounce packaged onion soup mix

Directions

Stir together yeast, warm water and 1-teaspoon sugar in a large bowl. Let it set for 5 to 10 minutes then transfer to large bowl. Stir in 2 cups of water, the remaining sugar, salt, margarine, 61/4 cups of flour and soup mix. Combine until the dough forms, adding remaining flour a little bit at a time if needed. Put on a lightly floured surface. Knead until dough is smooth and elastic for about 7 minutes. Oil a large bowl and place the dough in it, turning it to coat it. Cover the bowl with a damp cloth and set in a warm place for 30 minutes to rise. Divide the dough in half and shape it into loaves and place it into 2 greased bread pans. Set aside to rise for 30 minutes. Preheat oven to 375 degrees Fahrenheit. Bake for 40 minutes, or until the loaves test done and sound hollow when tapped on the bottom. Yields 2 loaves of bread.

Argentina

Matambre

Ingredients

2 beef sirloin steaks, 1 inch thick
½ garlic clove, crushed
1 cup red wine vinegar
1 teaspoon dried thyme
6 large carrots, quartered lengthwise
12 ounces of fresh spinach
4 hard-cooked, wedged large eggs
1 large onion, sliced in rings
3 teaspoons of chopped parsley
1 teaspoon of cayenne pepper
¼ cup of vegetable oil
2 ½ cups of beef stock
Water, salt and pepper

Directions

Prepare the beef by slicing each steak horizontally to within ½ inch of the opposite side. Fold open and place in a shallow dish, one on top of each other. Combine the garlic, vinegar and the thyme. Pour the mixture over the beef, cover and refrigerate for 6 hours to thoroughly marinate. Meanwhile, cook the carrots in salted water for 20 minutes or until nearly tender. Preheat the oven to 400 degrees Fahrenheit. Remove the beef from the marinade and pat dry with paper towels and place with each steak overlapping 2 inches. Pound the overlap together with a meat mallet. Spread the spinach over the entire surface. Arrange the cooked carrots crosswise over the spinach. Sprinkle with parsley, salt, red pepper, egg wedges and onion rings. Roll the beef and filling and tie with kitchen string at 3-inch intervals. Place in a large roasting pan and pour the oil over and around the beef stock. Cover and roast for 1 hour, adding more stock as needed. Cool 10 minutes and remove the string, slice the beef and strain the cooking liquid. This dish is normally served refrigerated with the beef very cold, which makes it easier for slicing and serving.

Alfajores Danubio
(Layered Sweet Pastry)

Ingredients

250 grams of ground almonds
300 grams of butter
225 grams of confectioner's sugar
1 lemon rind
Vanilla essence
3 eggs
Almond essence
¼ kilogram of plain flour

Directions

Beat the butter with the sugar and essences. Add the eggs one at a time. Incorporate the flour and the almonds and knead lightly. Place dough in the fridge for about ½ hour. Roll out the dough and cut out rounds. Bake for about 20 minutes on grease and floured baking sheets. Take 2 rounds and put them together with marmalade, melted chocolate or duice de leche, then you can also roll the wet edges in shaved coconut.

Daube

Ingredients

2-½ pounds rump roast (or leg of lamb)
6 whole garlic cloves
6 whole cardamom seeds
6 whole cloves
1 small eight ounce can tomato sauce
4 cups water
1-teaspoon salt
2 tablespoons white vinegar
4 medium potatoes, peeled and diced

Directions

Make 6 deep cuts with a sharp knife into the rump roast (or leg of lamb.) Each cut about 2 inches long. Fill each cut with one of each; a garlic, a clove, a cardamom and a garlic clove.

In a 12-quart pot, mix tomato sauce, water, salt and vinegar. Add the meat. Bring to a boil on high heat. Reduce heat to low and let cook covered for 1 to 2 hours, or until meat can be cut with a spoon. Turn meat over twice in the process. Add more water if needed. Add the potatoes. Let cook for another 30 minutes. Serve with cooked rice.

Canja

Ingredients

3 pounds boneless chicken
1 medium onion, chopped
6 cups chicken stock
¼ cup long grain rice
¾ cup tomatoes, peeled and diced
½ cup young carrots, peeled and diced
Salt
Ground black pepper
¾-cooked ham, diced
1 tablespoon chopped fresh parsley

Directions

To a large cook pot, add the chicken, onion and chicken stock. Bring to a simmer and cover. Cook over low heat until the chicken is tender, about 45 minutes. Lift the chicken out onto a platter and set aside. Strain the stock through a sieve and set over a bowl. Dispense with the solids and skim off as much fat as possible from the stock.

Rinse out the saucepan and return the stock to it. Add the rice, tomatoes and carrots to the stock. Season with salt and black pepper to taste. Bring to a simmer. Cook until the rice is tender, about 25 minutes.

When the chicken is cool enough to handle, cut it into strips of about ½ x 1-½ inches. Return the chicken to the soup with the ham and cook just long enough to heat through. Add the parsley and serve.

Moqueca De Peixe (Flounder Dish)

Ingredients

2 lb. Fillets of Sole, Flounder or any white fish cut into 2 inch pieces.
1 medium onion chopped
1 or 2 fresh hot chili peppers, seeded and chopped
2 medium tomatoes, peeled and chopped
1 clove garlic
1-teaspoon fresh coriander leaves
3 tablespoons lime or lemon juice
¼ cup dende or olive oil

Directions

Put the fish in a large bowl. In a blender or food processor combine the onion, chili pepper, tomatoes, garlic, coriander and salt to taste. Add the lime or lemon juice. Reduce to a puree and add to the fish, mixing lightly. Let stand for 1 hour. Transfer to a saucepan and add 6 tablespoons of water and half of the olive oil. Cover and simmer for about 5 minutes until the fish is done. Pour in the remaining oil and heat for 1 more minute. Serve with rice.

Moqueca

Ingredients

2 kilograms of fish (Grouper or Shark)
Lime drops
½ teaspoon salt
Ground black pepper
3 red peppers, sliced (rings)
1-kilogram ripe tomatoes sliced (round)
5 medium sized onions, sliced (rings)
2 tablespoons chopped coriander
3 tablespoons chopped parsley
3 tablespoons chopped chive
1 cup cooking oil
250 milligrams coconut milk

Directions

Cut the fish into thick slices, season with lime, salt and pepper. Let sit in refrigerator for 1 hour. In a bowl, mix the red peppers, onions and tomatoes. Add coriander, parsley and chive. Mix well and spread some of the mixture over the bottom of a large pan. Pour the cooking oil and cook on top of the oven at low heat for 30 minutes. Turn oven off, cover tightly and let stand for 2 hours. Turn the oven on, when the dish starts to boil, add the coconut milk. Cook for 15 more minutes. Taste to see if fish is well cooked. Serve with white rice. Some use a light wine or water instead of cooking oil.

Brazilian Spiced Shrimp

Ingredients

6 Medium dried crushed malagueta chiles or piquins
3 tablespoons of olive oil
1 small onion chopped
2 stalks celery chopped
6 cloves garlic chopped
1-cup pimiento chopped
4 cups small shrimp peeled
2 medium tomatoes chopped
1-cup coconut milk
1-tablespoon liquid oil
½ teaspoon cinnamon
¼ teaspoon ground cloves
¼ teaspoon ground ginger
3 tablespoons lemon juice
Salt & pepper
¼ cup chopped cilantro

Directions

Soak chilies in hot water for 15 minutes then drain. Heat oil and sauté onions until soft. Add celery, garlic, chilies and pimiento. Sauté for 5 minutes, stir in the shrimp and sauté until pink. Remove from heat and put shrimp aside in a holding pan. Return original pan to stove. Combine tomatoes, coconut milk, palm oil and spices and bring to a boil. Reduce heat and simmer until mixture thickens, about 10 minutes. Return shrimp, stir in lemon juice and season with salt and pepper. Garnish with cilantro and serve on rice.

Shrimp

Ingredients

Juice of 1 lemon
1 onion finely chopped
1 clove garlic minced
1 to 2 tablespoons white vinegar
½ teaspoon salt
1 pound fresh shrimp, shelled and deveined
1-teaspoon fresh cilantro chopped
2 tablespoons tomato paste Black pepper to taste
1 cup thin coconut milk
½ cup thick coconut milk
2 to 3 tablespoons oil

Directions

Marinate the shrimp in the lemon, onion, garlic, vinegar and salt for 30 minutes. Put mixture into a saucepan and add cilantro, tomato paste and black pepper to taste. Add thin coconut milk and cook over low heat until the shrimp are cooked. Add the thick coconut milk and oil. Continue cooking for another 5 minutes, Serve with rice.

Fish With Young Ginger

Ingredients

750 gram of fish
125 gram of fresh young root of ginger
One lemon's juice
2 tablespoons of peanut oil
1-tablespoon sesame oil
6 cloves of garlic, thin sliced.
3 tablespoons of sesame seed
2 tablespoons soy sauce

Directions

Wash and scale fish. Scrape the skin off the ginger and slice very thin and cut slices into thread-like slivers. Marinate ginger in strained lemon juice while preparing the remaining items.

Heat the oils in a small pan and fry garlic slowly, do not burn. Color should be pale gold. Pour the oil and garlic over the ginger. In the same pan, dry fry the sesame seeds until golden brown. Add the ginger/garlic mixture. Add soy and mix well and sprinkle over the fish fillets. Steam in individual foil packages for 15 minutes. Then you enjoy.

Canary Islands

Breakfast Dish

Ingredients

4 slices of bread from a large loaf (1/4 inch thick)
9 ounces of blueberries or black berries
4 eggs
¾ pint milk
1-teaspoon vanilla essence
3-tablespoon sugar
1 ounce flaked almonds

Directions.

Preheat the oven to 375 degrees. Cut the bread into chunks and place on a baking sheet and bake for about 10 minutes until lightly browned then let cool. Beat together the eggs, milk, vanilla essence and sugar. Place the toasted cubes and blueberries in a buttered shallow ovenproof dish and pour over the egg mixture. Sprinkle with the flaked almonds and let set for 30 minutes. Bake for about 40 minutes until golden brown. Serve hot with plain yogurt.

China

Mapo Tofu

Ingredients

2 tablespoons oil to sauté
1-tablespoon black bean garlic salt
1-teaspoon red chili paste with garlic
¼ pound ground pork
1 package fresh tofu cut into cubes
¼ cup chopped green onions
Salt

Directions

In a deep pan or wok, place the oil, sauces and ground port, turning the fire to high, gradually combining meat and sauces as the heat grows. When the meat browns and is cook all the way through, turn to medium fire and then add the tofu. Mix gently and simmer for 5 to 7 minutes, stirring occasionally until well blended and the tofu is hot. Add green onion and toss, adding salt to taste.

Columbia

Humintas

Ingredients

3 Packages frozen corn thawed
½ cup skimmed milk
1 & 2/3 cups yellow corn meal
2 tablespoons sugar
1-teaspoon baking powder
1-teaspoon salt
½ teaspoon anise seeds
¼ cup raisins
¼ teaspoon ground cinnamon
1 large egg
2 large egg whites
4 ounces thinly sliced Muenster cheese
½ teaspoon paprika

Directions

Preheat the oven to 350 degrees Fahrenheit. Spray a 9-inch baking pan with vegetable oil cooking spray. In a blender or food processor, in 2 batches, puree the corn and milk until smooth. In a large mixing bowl, sift together the corn meal, sugar, baking powder, salt, anise seeds, cinnamon and raisins. In a small bowl beat the egg and egg whites together. Stir the beaten eggs and the corn puree into the dry ingredients until just moistened. Spoon the batter into the prepared pan and cover the top with cheese. Sprinkle with paprika. Bake 40 to 45 minutes until a knife inserted in the center comes out clean. Cool for 20 minutes before cutting into 9 square pieces.

Green Mealie Bread

Ingredients

2 cups ground green mealies (raw corn)
2 cups flour
2 tablespoons sugar
1-teaspoon salt
4 teaspoons baking powder
Cold water

Directions

Mix dry ingredients together. Add enough water to form a stiff dough. Put the mixture into a greasy loaf pan and steam for about 1-½ hours. Makes a one pound loaf.

Squash With Peanuts

Ingredients

1 cup roasted peanuts
2 tablespoons peanut oil
5 cups cooked squash
Salt
White or brown sugar or honeybee honey

Directions

Chop the shelled peanuts coarsely. Add squash to oil and salt to taste. Heat slowly for about 15 minutes. Serve hot topped with white or brown sugar or honeybee honey. Serves four.

Green Papaya Jam

Ingredients

3 cups sugar
3 cups water
3 cups green papayas, grated
½ teaspoon vanilla
Juice of one lemon (1 tablespoon)

Directions

Heat sugar and water for about 5 minutes until syrup is formed. Add grated papayas and cook slowly over low heat. When mixture thickens, remove from heat and add vanilla and lemon juice. Mix well and pour into jars and seal. Fills two large jars.

Croatia

Dalmatian Fritters

Ingredients

7 ounces flour
3 egg yolks
Salt
1-tablespoon sugar
1-tablespoon sour cream
2 tablespoons rum
Powdered sugar
1 sachet vanilla sugar
Frying oil

Directions

Sift the flour, Wisk the egg yolks together with a pinch of salt. Make a depression in the heaped flour, pour in the whisked egg yolks, cream or smetana and rum and knead into a firm pastry. Cover and set aside for 30 minutes and then roll out thinly. Using a fluted pastry-cutting wheel, cut into strips, shaping them as desired. Fry them in hot oil.

Janjeca Juha (Lamb)

Ingredients

14 ounces of lamb meat
1-bunch root vegetables
2 ounces of rice
2 ounces of savoy cabbage
2 egg yolks
2 cloves garlic
1 onion
1 bay leaf
4 or 5 pepper corns
Juice of 1 lemon
4 ounces sour cream
Salt and pepper
Parsley
1 Tablespoon of mixed spices

Directions

Thoroughly wash the meat and vegetables and cut into cubes. Cut the savoy cabbage into strips. Mix the egg yolks with the sour cream and lemon juice. Chop the parsley. Place the meat in a fair amount of water and bring to a boil. Skim well; add cubed vegetables, onion garlic cloves, bay leaf, salt, pepper and spices. Boil the cabbage separately. Cook rice in salted water, drain and rinse well under cold water. As soon as the meat is tender, strain the soup and set the meat and vegetables aside. Slowly add the egg yolk, sour cream, and etc. mixture to the soup, stirring constantly. Then add the rice, meat and vegetables and sprinkle with chopped parsley.

El Salvador

Kumquat Refrigerator Pie

Ingredients

2/3 cups pureed kumquats
1 – 9" baked piecrust
1 small container of cool whip
1 can of condensed milk
½ cup of lemon juice

Directions

Just beat the milk and whipped topping together, then add the lemon juice and beat until it thickens, Pour in the kumquats, beat some more and then pour it into the pie shell and chill it for several hours to firm it up.

Greenland

Vanillekranse (Cookies)

Ingredients

500 grams flour
400 grams butter
300 grams powdered sugar
1 egg
Seeds of vanilla bean

Directions

Mix everything together and knead until smooth (add a little water if necessary.) Roll into rolls about 7 mm thick. Cut the rolls into 8 cm long pieces and form each piece into a ring. Arrange a layer of cookies on a greased cooking plate with a little space between them. Bake the cookies on the middle rack of the oven at 210 C for about 6 minutes.

Duice de Leche (Honduran Dessert)

Ingredients

1 bottle milk
1 lb. Sugar
2 sweet bread rolls
2 egg yolks
Cinnamon to taste

Directions

Cook the milk together with the sugar and cinnamon and stir. When it begins to thicken, add bread crumbs (very finely crumbled) and continue stirring. When it reaches the desired texture, remove from heat and beat thoroughly. While it is still warm, add the well-beaten eggs yolks and let it cool.

Indonesian Sate

Ingredients

4 chicken breasts cut in 1" cubes. (Can also use beef, pork or shrimp)
12 bamboo skewers (soak in water 15 to 30 minutes to prevent burn before broiling)
Marinade the following
2 cloves garlic, crushed
½ teaspoon each of ground coriander, cumin, tumeric or 1 ½ teaspoons curry powder
3 macadamia nuts crushed
¼ cup kecap manis (sweet soy sauce)
¾ cup coconut milk
½ teaspoon trasi (blachan) or 1 teaspoon shrimp paste
1 stalk lemon grass, peeled crushed and sliced
Red chilies (optional)

Directions

Sprinkle chicken with salt and pepper to taste, then soak in marinade for at least 2 hours or overnight. Thread 5 to 6 chicken cubes to a skewer or put under broiler. Serve with peanut sauce.

Peanut Sauce

Ingredients

½ cup peanut butter, 2 cloves garlic, minced
4 shallots, chopped fine
1-cup water or coconut milk
2 tablespoons kecap (sweet soy sauce)
½ teaspoon tarsi (shrimp paste)
2 tablespoons tamarind or lemon juice
1-tablespoon brown sugar
1-teaspoon brown sugar
1-teaspoon sambal or chili powder
Salt to taste
2 tablespoons kecap

Directions

Dilute peanut butter with liquid. Add spices and cook for 5 minutes or until sauce thickens.

Lapis Surabaya (Pound Cake)

Ingredients

570 cc egg yolk (approximately 30 eggs)
2 egg whites
350 gram butter, mixed on high speed until contents rise and color turns white
120 gram all purpose flour
450 gram granulated sugar
20 gram powdered milk (If desired you can substitute with 20 grams of all purpose flour)
1 tablespoon chocolate paste or cocoa
½ teaspoon vanilla
1-tablespoon rum paste for fragrance and flavor (Or two tablespoons rum)

Directions

Using high speed, mix together egg yolks, sugar, vanilla and rum paste until mixture thickens and color turns white, it usually takes about 10 minutes. Don't under mix, as the batter won't rise when baked. Fold in the flour, then add the pre-whisked butter and mix well. Divide the mixture into 3 separate bowls. Add chocolate paste or cocoa in one and yellow coloring in the other two. Coloring is optional. Most bakeries use it for appearance to make the cake look delicious. Preheat the oven to 200 degrees Celsius or 400 degrees Fahrenheit. Grease a 11-inch round cake pan with butter or Crisco shortening and pour in the batter mix until it is half filled. Bake until the sides moves away from the baking pan. A toothpick test should come out clean when done. Let cool before stacking the layers. You can use fruit spreads or icing for layering the cake. Drain the juices from the fruit spread before layering to prevent sogging the cake.

Semur Daging (Sliced Beef)

Ingredients

1 lb. Beef roast, thinly sliced
2 shallots, sliced
1 clove garlic, finely chopped
2 teaspoons kecap manis (sweet soy sauce)
2 tablespoons butter
2 hardboiled eggs, halved
2 potatoes, thinly sliced
2 tomatoes, peeled and chopped
4 scallions, chopped
Salt and pepper to taste
Pinch of nutmeg
Thinly sliced fried onion

Directions

Fry shallots and garlic in butter until lightly browned. Add meat and potato slices and sauté briefly. Add the tomato, soy sauce, salt, pepper and nutmeg. Mix well. Cover and cook for 5 minutes. Add eggs and cook for 5 minutes more. Add scallions just prior to serving and garnish with fried onions. Serve with white rice.

Chili

Ingredients

2 pounds minced beef
1 onion finely chopped
2 garlic clove crushed
7 green chili peppers
1-tablespoon olive oil
1-tablespoon flour
1-tablespoon chili powder
1-teaspoon ground cumin
4 tomatoes
1 teaspoon mixed spices
Salt
Freshly ground black pepper
Water

Directions

Heat oil in a large saucepan, add onion, garlic and chili ingredients and heat until golden and tender. Remove and set aside. Add the flour, stir in. Add the chili powder and cumin, cook for 3 minutes, stir constantly. Add the tomatoes and cooked onion, garlic and chili. Add enough water to cover mixture. Increase the heat and bring to a boil, stir constantly. Reduce heat and simmer on a low heat for 150 minutes. Season with salt and pepper and sprinkle with spices to garnish.

Nigeria

Jollof Rice

Ingredients

One pound of chicken
½ lb. Beef, ham or bacon
¼ cup of flour
1 medium onion, chopped
½ cup cooking oil
1 small can tomato paste
2 cups of rice
1 package frozen mixed vegetable
3 cups of water
Salt and pepper to taste

Directions

Cut up chicken, beef, ham and bacon Season with salt and pepper. Heat ½ cup of oil in a pan, sauté one medium chopped onion. Then add ½ pound of ham or bacon meat that is smoked, ½ cup of bleached flour and one small can of partially dehydrated tomato paste. Stir well, then place cover on pot and simmer with one additional cup of water for one hour. Add two additional cups of water, salt and pepper to your taste and bring to a boil. Add one pound of chicken and two cups of rice and simmer until rice is done. Add one package of mixed vegetables 5 minutes before removing the chicken-rice mixture from the fire.

Pakistan

Vegetable Jalfrasie

Ingredients

1 large onion
2 mild green peppers
2 large tomatoes
½ pound broccoli
½ pound cauliflower
4 tablespoons butter
1 teaspoon red chili powder
½ teaspoon turmeric
1-inch stick of ginger
3 cloves of garlic
2 tablespoons white vinegar
2 tablespoons tomato puree

Directions

Chop the onion, cut green peppers, tomatoes, broccoli and cauliflower into 1-inch cubes. Melt butter and sauté onion. Add all the remaining vegetables and stir-fry for about 5 minutes over medium heat. Add the spices and vinegar. Stir in the tomato puree and simmer for about 5 minutes. Season to taste and with salt and fresh ground pepper.

Peruvian Roasted Chicken

Ingredients

2 ½ tablespoons garlic powder
1 tablespoon plus 1-teaspoon ground cumin
4 tablespoons white vinegar
2 ½ tablespoons paprika
2 teaspoons freshly ground black pepper
3 tablespoons white wine
3 tablespoons soya or canola oil
¾ teaspoon salt
1 - 3 to 4 pound chicken
Juice of 1 lemon, mixed with 1-quart cold water

Directions

In medium sized bowl, mix first eight ingredients. Wash chickens thoroughly with lemon water and remove excess fat from inside chickens. With a large carving fork, poke deep holes all over the chicken, including under the wings. Rub the marinade thoroughly inside and outside the chicken. Seal chicken in a large plastic bag and marinate for at least 2 hours (but preferably up to 24 hours) in your chiller. Remove chicken from the bag and dilute marinade left behind with a tablespoon of water. Place the chicken on a rotisserie spit and roast at a medium heat for 45 to 55 minutes.

If broiling, cut chicken in half lengthwise and broil for 30 to 40 minutes, basting with marinade every 10 minutes.

Russia Egg Salad

Ingredients

6 hard-boiled eggs
150 ml. Mayonnaise
5 tablespoons sour cream
1 small clove garlic crushed
¼ teaspoon hot mustard
¼ teaspoon salt
2 tablespoons finely chopped spring, onion or chives
1 small carrot

Directions

Slice the eggs thinly. Mix the mayonnaise, sour cream, garlic, mustard and salt. Spread the eggs out in an oval serving dish, cover with mayonnaise mix. Sprinkle the chopped spring onions on top. Garnish with grated carrot.

Musaka (Beef Caserole)

Ingredients

1 kilogram potatoes
400 grams ground meat
1 large onion chopped
4 eggs
3-deciliter milk
Salt
Pepper
Oil

Directions

Heat oil in pan. Add onion and cook until it gets golden brown. Add meat salt and rich quantity of pepper. Fry until meat gets brown. Remove the pan from heat. Cut potatoes in slices as for chips, but not that thin (about 2-3 mm.) Put 2 teaspoons of salt in potatoes and mix well. In casserole put oil, then potatoes until it covers the bottom. Put meat to cover potatoes and then potatoes again. Mix 4 eggs in a bowl, add milk, mix well and pour in potatoes and meat and put in oven for about 40 minutes or until potatoes on the top gets brown.

Welfenpudding

Ingredients

½ liter milk
120 grams sugar
1 packet vanilla (about one large spoon)
One dash salt
40-gram cornstarch
4 eggs, set whites and yokes apart
250 ml dry white wine
1 large spoon lemon juice
10-gram cornstarch for later

Directions

Beat egg whites until very stiff. Mix 40 grams corn starch with about 3 large spoons milk. The vanilla, sugar, salt and remainder of milk should be brought to a boil. Add the cornstarch and milk mixture and bring back to a boil, always stirring. Take off heat and slowly fold egg whites in with only wooden spoon until completely mixed. Take care not to flatten egg whites with strong folding, be gentle. Fill Mixture in only a glass bowl (so color can be seen by guests) and cool completely.

Now For Topping
Combine the egg yolks, 80 grams of sugar, lemon juice and slightly mix the cornstarch with some wine and add that too. Bring slowly to a boil over medium heat. Then pass through a strainer to remove any chunks of cornstarch and pour on top of the pudding.

Ukraine

Piroshkises

Ingredients

½ cup chopped onion
¼ cup margarine
8 oz. chopped mushrooms
¾ teaspoon salt
14 teaspoons pepper
1 hard cooked egg yolk
1 piecrust mix
1-cup sour cream

Directions

Sauté onions until tender and then add the margarine. Add mushrooms and then sauté 3 minutes. Stir in salt, pepper and egg yolk. Cool then combine piecrust and sour cream to make dough. Roll out 1/8 inch thick. Cut in 3-inch rounds. Place 1 teaspoon filling in center, fold and press edges together. Bake at 350 degrees for 12 – 15 minutes. Makes 40 and can be frozen.

TESTIMONIES

Below are a few of the hundreds of testimonies I have received from radio listeners and students from around the world. I have omitted their names and exact locations for their privacy and protection. Please pray for these precious people, of who many are facing severe persecution.

April 10, 2007

My 25-day-old daughter got sick and died in my arms. She received improper CPR by a neighbor causing several injuries throughout her tiny body. She was 7 lbs. and 20 inches long. I was arrested on April 11, 2007. Charged with causing the injuries that caused her death on her death on April 12, 2007 at 7:29 p.m. Mom pulled the plug on life support. D.A. came after me, tried me, and found guilty and sentenced to 20 years at the TDCJ. I am currently 12 years on this 20-year sentence. All for a crime I did not do. I couldn't afford legal counsel. I was saved on May 17, 2007.

U.S. Prison Inmate

****

The Gospel Of Matthew told me enough for me to want to give my life to the Lord. I began my journey with the strong desire to share whatever I had learned with everyone I knew and came across. Sadly that fire burned out due to not being fueled. Over the years the same has continued to transpire-very highs and lows. It has continued to be my desire to learn to rest completely in thought's provisions. This course has truly helped me to see why getting off course has been so easy for me. Thank you for your ministry.

U. S. Prison inmate:

****

Dr. Johnny Woodard:

A surprising and welcome discovery of the Bible is this, "God uses failures like me. Grace by definition means that God gives us what we don't deserve and could never earn. And though we may fail, underneath us are God's open arms. Jesus spoke to them at once, "Don't be afraid" He said: "Take courage I am here." Matthew 14:27. With nowhere else to turn, I went down on my knees and cried, "God, I can't do this prison sentence, please help me." It was only then that a glimmer of light began to touch my heart, and then a willingness emerged to let God control my life. Would you be so kind to send me your Bible Study and I can get a free Bible when I am done?

I guess when you hit rock bottom you can only look up, huh? I learned that my tears weren't weakness, but my tears were a gift from God to ease the pain and hurt. Thank you for your time and have a blessed day.

U. S. Prison Inmate

****

My 13 year old was shot and killed by an 11-year-old boy and I gave up on God, asking why and even hating Him. I lost trust and faith in Him then and I was out of control with drugs and a bad lifestyle, ignoring my three daughters and grandkids. Then I committed a crime and came to prison, where I was born again. I have God in my life now. He has given me a peace and helped to forgive the boy who killed my son. He is here to comfort and protect me. I thank you Jesus for being my Saviour.

U. S. Prison Inmate

****

I lost a sister to a drunk driver. She was my only sister and was very close to me. I didn't know how to handle it. I asked Christ to help me overcome. He has helped me understand, told me to forgive the accuser. So much has happened over the years, such as losing my parents and being alone, that I call upon Christ all the time. He is such a blessing and all I need everyday.

U. S. Prison Inmate

I was a wicked man, addicted to porn and alcohol. Despite being molested at a young age, I never forgave those involved. I got really deep into porn and was arrested and still remained unchanged. After two months I found myself in solitary confinement. Shortly after, they put another guy in there with me in a one-man cell. He had a Bible, so I borrowed it and read the whole Bible in two weeks. I asked Jesus into my heart on June 26, 2011. I started Bible studies and really wanted my life to change. I was baptized on July 26, 2012 and I've been serving my Lord & Saviour, Jesus Christ, for I am His humble, lowly servant.

U. S. Prison Inmate

****

I was born in a Thailand Christian family and thought being born in a Christian family made me a Christian. When I found myself in prison for a crime I did not commit, I tried to get closer to God. I found a place in the Bible in John 3:1-6 when Jesus told Nicodemus unless one is born again he cannot see the kingdom of Heaven, it was then that I realized that only by being born again can I become a Christian. I realized that I needed to ask Jesus to come into my life as my Lord and Saviour. I then prayed and ask Jesus to come into my heart, as I confessed my sins to Him.

Thailand

****

Since I have given my life to God, I have come to forsake all the bad things I used to do that do not please God, like lying and making filthy statements. Now I preach the good news to others who do not know about God and are eager to know Christ.

Thailand

I was walking around the prison yard feeling down and out and I asked God if He was real to come to me. A couple of minutes later a guy came up to me and asked me if I knew Jesus and I said "No, but I think I would like to. Later that day, I placed my faith in Jesus and what He did for me on the cross. Soon, it seemed every Christian that was in the yard came up to me and welcomed me into the family.

U. S. Prison Inmate

****

I weighed 93 pounds, was strung out, homeless, starved, lost my job and my kids and my family. I went to jail and was about dead, was on emergency watch for 11 days. During that time I realized God has saved my life and I hit my knees and cried and thanked him for saving me. I started reading my Bible and on 7/19/15 I was baptized.

U. S. Prison Inmate

****

To put it simply, Jesus came and saved me at the darkest moment of my life. A time when whiskey, women and drugs was my trinity.

U. S. Prison Inmate

****

I had been in the church from about the age of 9 to 18 and then in and out until I was 34. I was arrested on October 23rd and finally realized that I needed Jesus Christ in my life. I am now serving a sentence of 15 years to life for the second-degree murder of a friend that I murdered in a state of drunkenness that I honestly don't remember doing. But I have to thank God for not taking me while living in my sins. I believe I will go home to my children and grandchildren someday and I want to show them the life my mom wanted for me before she passed away 20 years ago at the age of 34. I am now 39 years of age and my children are living for God and also giving my grandchildren the foundation they need in their lives.

I thank you and everyone that brings the Word Of God to us inmates. Even for those who will never see the streets again, they can be free on the inside with Jesus Christ.

U. S. Prison Inmate

****

Dear Brother Johnny Woodard,
Thank you for you sent me your Bible College Course and Tracts as you told me. Yesterday I received safely my beloved Brother. Your Bible Course and Book is very wonderful so I will select 25 Bible College Students and I will start again Grace Bible College soon because this year our Grace Bible College stopped, so please pray for our 25 bible college students weekly.

India

****

Dear Dr. Johnny Woodard
Greetings to you in Jesus name.

I am from Bangladesh and am an ex Muslim and have a small ministry to the Muslims and Hindus here. Recently I have seen your ministry website and the excellent work you doing for His glory. Bangladesh needs help with the Word of God and I will be happy if you start your course for my nation in Bengali. I am happy to help your program here. Please pray about it and let me know with the guidance of God.

Much blessing to you always.
Bangladesh

****

Dear Dr. Johnny,

Greetings to you in Jesus name, Amen. Thank you so much for your love and care to help poor Nigerian with Bibles freely. I received two boxes of Bibles today with tracts and eyeglasses, what a great blessing. We are blessed of your love and faithfulness in sending us Bibles monthly.

Nigeria

****

I was in the middle of a 5-acre field and it was about 11:30 pm and it was pouring down rain. I dropped to my knees and I asked God for something that I needed that I had never asked for before, and that was His Son, Jesus Christ.

U. S. Prison Inmate

****

I gave my life to the Lord at a young age because I had a Godly mother who made sure that all her children grew up knowing the love of the Lord.

P.S. These have been wonderful lessons that lead you through the Bible and show you the love of Christ. Thank you for what you do to lead others to Christ.

U. S. Prison Inmate

Hello, how great it was to locate your email. I graduated from the college in 2005 with a diploma. I'm now a pastor doing hospital ministry. I visit the hospital every Sunday and lead people to Christ, pray for their sicknesses and give out eggs, bananas and sweets. Thanks for training me. I started the ministry in 2005 and I am doing it until today. This afternoon I was there and preached in the surgery wards. I have a team of about 20 members who accompanied me to the wards.

May God bless you. Amen.

Africa

****

I wanted to thank you for your Bible Study. The Holy Spirit has used it to convict me and also teach me many things. I have been pretending. I considered using faith to get what I felt like I deserved. I hope this is not the last lesson because I enjoy them. I just want you to know how much of an impact these lessons have made on me.

U. S. Prison Inmate

****

When I was out in the world I was drifting farther off course from God. When I got to prison February of 2014 I came closer to God. On 5/31/14 I went to a service and I felt like the preacher was speaking to me, so after the service he asked is anyone who wasn't saved to come forward and I did.

U. S. Prison Inmate

****

I am 45 years old and I grew up attending a Fundamental Independent Baptist Church, as well as their Christian School. I accepted Jesus as my Saviour, was baptized by immersion in 1989. Since then I have surrendered my life to preach and went to the Hiles-Anderson Bible College in Indiana. I lost my focus and got off course and came to prison in 2004 and will be released in 2021. I would like to get my life back inline with God's will and honor my commitment to preach. I would love to hear from you concerning this matter. I love your course, Amen and am enjoying it. It is very informative and in line with God's Word.

Thank you

U. S. Prison Inmate

****

Dear Johnny,

Greetings to you in Jesus name, Amen. Thank you so much for your message, what a great blessing to receive your Boxes of Bibles, Tracts and Eye Glasses last month and last week Friday. I have been so busy in the bush; we just build and dedicated a new Church Building at Ikhueniro Community, Benin City. I will send you update shortly with more photos.

Nigeria

****

My 13 year old was shot and killed by an 11-year-old boy and I gave up on God, asking why and even hating Him. I lost trust and faith in Him then and I was out of control with drugs and a bad lifestyle, ignoring my three daughters and grandkids. Then I committed a crime and came to prison, where I was born again. I have God in my life now. He has given me a peace and helped to forgive the boy who killed my son. He is here to comfort and protect me. I thank you Jesus for being my Saviour.

U. S. Prison Inmate

****

I lost a sister to a drunk driver. She was my only sister and was very close to me. I didn't know how to handle it. I asked Christ to help me overcome. He has helped me understand, told me to forgive the accuser. So much has happened over the years, such as losing my parents and being alone, that I call upon Christ all the time. He is such a blessing and all I need everyday.

Praise Jesus!
U. S. Prison Inmate

****

Dear Dr. Woodard D-D

My heart is filled with gratitude, I am truly overwhelmed. I can't believe I actually did a Bible Correspondence Course. I did the best I can. I always wanted to do this, but finances would not allow me. I must say, God's richest continued blessings to you and yours. I must confess also, when I realized I had finished, tears came to my eyes, tears of joy and satisfaction. From the depths of my heart, God bless you.

Trinidad, West Indies
You have made me a better person.

****

Dr. Johnny Woodard
The Bread Of Life Institute
Kirbyville, Texas

Dear brother in the Lord:

Greetings in the love of Jesus Christ, the founder and maker of love. He first loved us and gave His life for us and makes us to copy from Him. Thank God for His love, kindness and compassion toward the world.

Happiness behind sorrow.

Happiness comes when we started your lessons, the way you present your good presentation of the gospel made us move into remote pagan villages, where they believe in their father's idols of wooden gods. We went to idol god worshippers' villages, just to present to them the good news of Jesus Christ and free salvation that He gave to all who believe in Him, who do not need goats and hen's killing anymore. God, in the free pardon of sin, has purchased them by the blood of Jesus Christ. If anyone accepts Christ Jesus as his or her personal Saviour, they are free from sin.

Hearing this, many accepted Jesus Christ by lifting their hands and we gave them an invitation to come out. We told them that they will not worship idols anymore and they will not kill any goats and hens anymore for their idol gods. That is when riots started; some of us were beaten to death because we wanted to destroy their father's false god. Please pray for us, we are ready to go back to the villages when we are well. Please pray for us and the villages to help us win them for Christ Jesus.

We are using your teaching to prove to the villagers that God is still in action. Please, we like your teaching, is your church teaching the same also? How many students do you have in Nigeria? We want to follow your teaching, it is easy to understand. No church here will accept this pure truth teaching. When hearing from you, we will write more. Thanks for your good teaching. Thanks for love and kindness. Please be with us to spread your teachings.

Yours in Christ:

Notice:

We accept to die for Christ sake, for His true teaching, that has not mixed the name of God with idol gods. We are to point out to them truth about God and the gods of wood. We want them to know that God Almighty is the maker of the earth and all things that are on the earth. We did not have the right teaching to lay our hands on. But now, your teaching shows us the right teaching. Please, please, be with us. Let the light shine in darkness.

Write us soon
Nigeria, West Africa

****

Dear Brethern:

I sincerely thank you for the thoughtfulness and diligent kindness in sending me the materials I got from your prestigious Biblical Institute. No words can express my deepest gratitude to you for the assistance you've been giving me by sending the two books of God's word. Whenever I read the books, I feel a fresh fire or zeal and commitment to follow Jesus, to love Him and to love all mankind. Your books which you sent me stand for the big part of my Spiritual growth and maturity. It has been a blessing to me and now I thirst and hunger, yearn for it like physical food because it is infinitely nourishing.

I praise the Lord for your ministry of Jesus Christ. I don't want to be obedient in a religious way as the Pharisees were, but I want to be obedient from my heart with love. Keep pressing in, keep spreading the word, keep walking in love and I will keep you before the throne of grace. I'm thankful to every one of you in nurturing my soul. Christ gives me a continuing life of service and strengthens me to stand firm in bad situations. Please pray for me because I am jobless, I need your prayers!!!!!!!!!!!!!!!!!!!!!!!!!!!!!!

My offering for what you are doing in my sincere prayers is that God will supply your needs. I believe that soon I'll be able to do more than this. May our Heavenly Father bless you in grace and your worldwide ministry abundantly. In anticipation of an early reply, I'm looking forward to hearing from you soon.

Algeria

****

Dear Dr. Johnny Woodard:

A warm "hello" to you my brother in Christ. I am 15 years old. I was born last December 29, 1992. I'm the second oldest child in our family. I'm very thankful to God because I have been given the opportunity to be a student through your correspondence school. If you only knew the great change that has happened in my life. Bible reading becomes our hobby. I and my younger brothers and sisters became knowledgeable in God's word. Reading the great Bible question and answer book from the Old and New Testaments woke an interest. Praying every day is part of our daily life. I'm sorry if I mail this test back to you delayed. It's just because I don't have enough money to pay on the delivery of my letters to the post office. I need to look for a job here to pay the delivery bill given by the postman. Most of our fellowmen are suffering poverty that even buying our needs, like clothing, slippers and rice, we can't afford to buy any more. I hope you understand our situation.

I'm looking forward to the Advanced Course 2 (The New Testament Church), so that I can finish all the course and receive my diploma immediately. I'll close this letter here. Hope to hear from you soon.

Always:
Philippines

****

Dr. Woodard,

Praise GOD!!! We have received the lessons you sent us and have been blessed in our daily devotions and study. As we were reading them, some of our fellow believers have expressed interest in studying as well. Would you allow us to photocopy the material you have sent us?

Your fellow servant,
The Philippines

****

Greetings in the Name of our Saviour Jesus Christ!

I am happy to inform you that I already finished the Advance course study you've sent last year. Really it's a blessing for me to have the opportunity to study and be a part of your Bible Correspondence Course. I already sent my answer sheets last week, and I am sorry for I haven't sent them earlier.

Thank you so much for helping me study the Word of God in a deeper sense. Somehow it answers the many questions I have in life. I would like also to inquire if I can take your Basic Bible Course as well? I am looking forward to hearing from you very soon.

Again, thank you so much and may God continue to bless you and your ministry richly. I will be praying that the Lord will continue to sustain and use your Bible Correspondence Course in helping many Christians to have a better understanding in the Word of God and God Himself and in reaching out many people who still don't know Christ in their lives. Your booklets are great and I find it very helpful.

Yours in Christ,
The Philippines

****

The Lord Bless:

I am so much happy to info you that the diploma you sent is at good hand, may the good Lord meet all your needs. I am so much thankful to the Lord for making it possible for me to go through this course, praise be to His name. Stay blessed in Jesus name,

Love from:
Ghana, West Africa

****

Dear Johnny

I wish to thank the Lord for making it possible for us to go through this Bible Correspondence Institute by the help of the good Lord with success. In fact, this lesson has given me a great eye opener into the word of God. Also I have learned new things in this lesson, which will help me in my mission work and church planting.

In fact, I have just started a new church in one of the new communities in Tema. So far I have (6) six disciples, so I hope to start Sunday services in the first Sunday of February 2008, so keep us in your prayers. Please, I have given your email address to a pastor friend in Liberia to write to you for the lessons. I hope you like it.

I am so sorry for the delay in sending in the last lesson for I went on a long mission trip and am now back to start a new church.

May the good Lord bless all that you are doing and meet all your needs. The soul-winning lesson was great. It is helping us train people to win souls for the Lord.

Ghana, West Africa

****

Dr Johnny Woodard D.D: President
The Bread of Life International
Bible Correspondence Institute
PO Box 334
Kirbyville, Texas 75956 USA

Dearest in the Lord,

    Object: COMPLETION OF THE ADVANCED COURSES AND INFORMATION

I continually praise the Name of the Lord for the tremendous work He has been doing through your Institute to equip the children of God with the Word of God and to spread the Gospel of Salvation throughout the world. May He continue to bless and strengthen you so that the Word can reach the more remote and unreachable places of the earth. Amen!

In fact, one month ago, I received some manuals (Advanced Courses 1-7) from your Institute as a student and I can affirm that these courses have been a blessing for me and the church I have the honor to pastor. This is to inform you that I have now completed all the courses and I will mail them to you tomorrow. And I will be expecting my diploma. Sorry for not having sent you the tests earlier. It was due to the fact that my schedule was very tied…

Furthermore, the main purpose for writing you this note is to enquire on: The possibility for us here to get French translation of your manuals because we are in a French speaking country and our people hardly speak English. In case this option is not possible, can we be granted the opportunity and privilege to get it translated into French for having a wider attendance (people enrolling as students)? I would also like to know whether you are not interested in creating a Regional Branch of The Bread of Life International Bible Correspondence Institute for French speaking people here in Côte d'Ivoire (West Africa) so that as many students as possible can profit from the so precious lessons contained in your various manuals (both Ordinary and Advanced Levels) I will be looking forward to hearing from you very soon.

Côte d'Ivoire , West Africa

****

Dear Dr. Woodard,

Heavenly greetings in the name of the Lord. I trust that all is well with you. I received the Course materials on Friday and am writing to say big thank you. I've finished reading thru the WITNESSING and I even quoted portions in my Sunday sermon at church. What a great support. Today, I started studying and answering the questions on SALVATION. In our part of the world, we don't get such materials easily and even the cost involved is so much that some of us can't easily buy. This is really SOLID MEAT. For example the portion about the trinity is so simple and that I can now conveniently preach it to the understanding of any person. Thank you. I wish to assure you and the brethren who support your ministry that they should continue to do it because only God knows the impact this material has on humanity ... including pastors and their congregations.

Doc, I have THREE leaders in my church who are true disciples and I would like to get copies for them and I will help them to study. Again below are addresses of some of my pastor friends who are also interested:

Nigeria, West Africa

****

Greetings,

I have just received the diploma you awarded me. I just wanted to say thank you and may God bless you. Maybe you would like to hear a little how I studied and completed your studies, glory to God. Let's see, I studied way (not a typo) into the night in some cases. I took them everywhere with me, and whenever I had the time I would sit down, ask God for guidance and begin. This included times when I would stay over night at church. I would get up early in the morning; I Even took them to summer church camp with me, hard to see a brother in the woods, studying to the glory of the Lord! I was deeply enriched by the study; I especially loved the study on the New Testament church. I pray God will be merciful enough to use me in any thing He sees fit, and I am glad I had the chance to gain valuable tools for His ultimate victory! To Him be the glory and the power forever AMEN!

God Bless your ministries until the rapture!
Hiroshima, Japan
Be bold, trust God.

****

Appreciation goes to The Bread Of Life International Bible Correspondence Institute for offering me this course and I pray God bless you abundantly.

I will not remain the same in witnessing Christ to the nation and this people around me.

Thanks:
Gulu, Uganda-East Africa

****

Greetings in the name of our LORD and Savior JESUS,

I have a 10-year-old daughter. I want her to receive your advance course one-salvation. She is attending Sunday school since two yrs old. And been active in music ministry, playing tambourine. But I noticed that as she grows her interests changes, I just want her to know GOD by heart and be equipped. I notice that she is interested in receiving mails, that's why I find it is a good start for her to study GODS WORD through mail, by the way I have been saved through this ministry, back in my high school years somebody enrolled me here and I learn more of God's word through this ministry.

The Philippines
Thank you and God Bless YOU and Your ministry.

****

Dear Brother in Christ. I have received your bible correspondence course. I like so much the course. And I have learned many new words about God. If it is in our Telugu Language so many people want to do this course. So many people can know about the word of God through this way. If you agree, I want to translate and co-ordinate your course in India.

India.

****

The Bread Of Life International
Bible Correspondence Institute
Dear Sir/Madam

I take an opportunity to read some brochure form 'THE BREAD OF LIFE' it was so thankful to in my life. I got an opportunity to learn about life, and Bible there for I would like to learn more about life, Jesus and Bible. Sir/Madam, If possible please I would like to request some brochure and 1 (one) bible below my address.

Awaiting early response.
Thanking you!
Yours faithfully
Dhaira, Dubai UAE

****

Dear Dr. Woodard,

I have completed the course sent to me. I am finding a possible way to send the answers to you. Our postal system is very slow and undependable. Indeed, I am blessed because your course has brought a great light and relief to most of my many doubts in the Bible. In the future I would like to suggest if you could appoint me in Liberia to oversee some of the students that would be willing to take this worthy course. Instead of posting to them individuals it can be posted to me and I will distribute them and after they complete they can bring them back to me for postage. It will real be revival in my country if even 10% of our pastors in the country gone through this course.

May the Lord richly bless you and all those whom are making it possible for such a rich lessons from the Word of God to reach to us in Africa.

Your student in the Lord,
Liberia

Dear Dr. Johnny:

I am so glad to write after having received the course on the 9th of November. It really shows that my wife and I will benefit a lot. We will study them prayerfully and carefully so as to grow in the Faith. About the picture, I will send to you anytime.

May God bless your efforts.
In Him:
Tanzania, East Africa

****

Dr Johnny Woodard:
Dear Sir:

I am so excited to reply you. I wasn't expecting this correspondence, it came as a surprise. I say thank you. This correspondence has really helped me. I wish the whole world had this message; there wouldn't be so much darkness.

Please always pray for me, that God would help me to preach this gospel to the end of the world. Thanking you in anticipation to my other programs to you.

Nigeria, West Africa

Please Check Out My Other Books Available Through My Publisher And Other Outlets In Different Formats.

Conclusion

As it takes time and the proper ingredients to prepare the recipes in this book, so does it take time and the proper ingredients to establish and build a successful ministry for the Lord. God's Word makes it very plain that we as believers are saved to serve God in whatever capacity He leads us to do so. Remember Paul's first words after his encounter with Jesus on the road to Damascus to arrest God's children there.

Acts 9:6 And he trembling and astonished said, Lord, what wilt thou have me to do? "And the Lord said unto him, Arise, and go into the city, and it shall be told thee what thou must do."

Note that the first words Paul said to Jesus was to ask Him what He (Jesus) wanted him to do. Note also that Jesus didn't ask Paul what he was interested in doing, He made it plain that He had a plan and purpose already for Paul's life.

Jesus told Paul what he "must do." God's plan for His servants has not changed since that fateful day many years ago, God instructs all of His children to be obedient to His will for their lives. It takes time and the needed resources for any ministry to be successful in God's eyes. My prayer for you is that this little book will encourage and motivate you to serve God out of a thankful heart for all the many blessings He bestows on all of His children.

Galatians 6:9 And let us not be weary in well doing: for in due season we shall reap, if we faint not.

www.ingramcontent.com/pod-product-compliance
Lightning Source LLC
LaVergne TN
LVHW021736060526
838200LV00052B/3307